THE REAL SUPERHEROES AND SUPERHEROINES!

What I want to be when I grow up!

by

SADAT KHAN

ILLUSTRATED BY LOWELL HILDEBRANDT

AuthorHouse™
1663 Liberty Drive
Bloomington, IN 47403
www.authorhouse.com
Phone: 1-800-839-8640

© 2010 Sadat Khan. All rights reserved.

No part of this book may be reproduced, stored in a retrieval system, or transmitted by any means without the written permission of the author.

First published by AuthorHouse 3/15/2010

ISBN: 978-1-4490-9281-8 (sc)

Library of Congress Control Number: 2010902548

Printed in the United States of America
Bloomington, Indiana

This book is printed on acid-free paper.

DEDICATION

This book is dedicated to Ameera and Azam, my niece and nephew who have brought me the joy and inspiration to compose this book!

"My special thanks goes to my parents Hamid and Momena for without them I would not have been who I am today and of course the rest of my family. A lot of special thanks also goes to Brandi, Bishop, Sam, Dennis and Margaret who I have learned a lot from and am grateful towards their inspiration of composing this book for the benefit of children. I wish that all children find hope, peace and prosperity with my writings."

.....Sadat Khan

"Three things I love to do when I read children a storybook is" :

A). Introduce the "title", the "author" and the "illustrator" before I even go on the first page. While doing that, I also ask if they know what the story could be all about, by exposing the front of the book. (Curiosity).

B). When the story reaches its centre point, I ask the children to predict what will happen next. (Prediction).

C). After reading the story I always ask children what their favorite part was. (Exercising memory).

"The more we ask and tell a child about a "story" they are about to get indulged into, the more they will open up and exercise their minds and imaginations towards a fun, prosperous and educational environment." ~~Sadat Khan.

"I don't want to go to the daycare mommy!" cried little Brandi, "I want to be with you!" "Now, now Brandi, remember, we talked about this so many times before! Don't you want to be a doctor and save people's lives when you grow up?" "Yes mommy," sobbed Brandi, "And so many people will be proud of you for trying to save lives every day, and you will be like a 'Superheroine' for them!" "However, right now mommy has to go save lives of people as those who are sick at the hospital because your mommy is a ……? "Super Nurse!" yelled little Brandi with so much joy.

"Who can tell me why it is so important to come to a daycare or preschool?" asked Mrs. Sultan, the teacher at "SuperKid's" Daycare. "Me, me, me!!" yelled all the children for they all knew that it is really important to come to school so that they can learn and grow up to be the "REAL Superheroes or Superheroines of our society. All the kids then gathered around Mrs. Sultan as she began to tell a beautiful story....

"Ok Tony, so tell me what do you want to be when you grow up?" "Voooooom!!" Flying his airplane that he built from the Lego blocks, he shouted out loud infront of the class, "I want to be an airplane pilot when I grow up!" infront of the whole class with great excitement as he flew his airplane he made from the Lego blocks. "And then I will become a "Super Pilot!!"

"What about you Brandi, what do you want to be when you grow up?" asked Mrs. Sultan. "I want to be a 'Super Doctor' and save people's lives when I grow up" as she pulled out her stethoscope from the doctors kit and put it near the heart of a teddy bear.

"How lovely!" exclaimed Mrs. Sultan. "Such lovely children I have in my class! You will all save our planet when you grow up and all of your parents and teachers will help you become those REAL Superheroes and Superheroines!" Maybe some of you would like to become a fireman or a police officer. "Who wants to be a fireman or a police officer?" " Me, me, me!!" shouted some of the children....

"Maybe some of you want to become a Businessman or a Businesswoman and make lots of money. Who wants to be a Businessman or a Businesswoman here?" asked Mrs. Sultan again. "Me, me, me!!" shouted some of the kids again; "or someone here wants to be a scientist or an engineer. Which one of you wants to be a scientist or an engineer kids?" asked Mrs. Sultan. And again the kids screamed with excitement, "Me, me, me!!" Or perhaps one of you wants to be a 'Super nurse' or a 'Super doctor' like little Brandi."

"Can any one here tell me what would happen if we did not go to schools and daycares? asked Mrs. Sultan. Then little Tony raised his hand and said, "I would not learn how to fly an airplane when I grow up and then I would crash it!" with a big frown on his face as he crashed his toy airplane that he made from his Lego blocks. "Very good answer Tony. I am so proud of you!" said Mrs. Sultan.

"And the same thing would be true for a train engineer or a ship captain, kids! If you don't go to school to learn how to drive a train or pilot a ship then you would either crash the train or sink the ship!!" said Mrs. Sultan. "Oh no!!" shouted little Bishop, looking a bit disappointed in the back of the class.....

Mrs. Sultan said, "Always remember children, the number one reason to come to a daycare or preschool is so we can learn things that can help us grow into someone really important and useful in life, just like all these REAL Superheroes or Superheroines we talked about today. Another good reason to come to daycares and preschools is so we can make a lot of friends and help save our planet TOGETHER with each others help as we grow up to be these REAL Superheroes or heroines."

"Oh, I don't want to crash my train or everyone in the train will get hurt Mrs. Sultan!" exclaimed little Bishop. "Don't worry Bishop. If you come to your daycare and then as you grow up to go to your other schools, you will learn perfectly how to drive a train in the right way and no one will then get hurt." Then Mrs. Sultan saw a big smile on Bishop's face and the entire class was very happy to learn why it is so important to come to a daycare or a preschool as it helps us to become someone really important and useful in our lives and the lives of others just like these REAL SUPERHEROES AND SUPERHEROINES!

THE END

LaVergne, TN USA
05 April 2010
178112LV00003B